ETTINSMOOR

RIVER SHRIBBLE

northern marsh

owlwood

BATTLE FIELD

witch's camp

N

aslan's camp

FORDS OF BERUNA

the stone table

RUSH RIVER

GALMA

dancing lawn

glasswater creek

stormness head

anvard

winding arrow river

...chenland

First published in Great Britain in 2005 by HarperCollins Children's Books. HarperCollins Children's Books is a division of HarperCollins Publishers Ltd.

1 3 5 7 9 10 8 6 4 2

Photographs by Tony Barbera, Phil Bray, Richard Corman and Donald M. McAlpine.

Activities by Sadie Chesterfield and Julia Simon-Kerr. Art by TK.

WALT DISNEY PICTURES AND WALDEN MEDIA PRESENT "THE CHRONICLES OF NARNIA: THE LION, THE WITCH AND THE WARDROBE" BASED ON THE BOOK BY C.S. LEWIS A MARK JOHNSON PRODUCTION AN ANDREW ADAMSON FILM MUSIC COMPOSED BY HARRY GREGSON-WILLIAMS COSTUME DESIGNER ISIS MUSSENDEN EDITED BY SIM EVAN-JONES PRODUCTION DESIGNER ROGER FORD DIRECTOR OF PHOTOGRAPHY DONALD M. McALPINE, ASC, ACS CO-PRODUCER DOUGLAS GRESHAM EXECUTIVE PRODUCERS ANDREW ADAMSON PERRY MOORE WALDEN MEDIA SCREENPLAY BY ANN PEACOCK AND ANDREW ADAMSON AND CHRISTOPHER MARKUS & STEPHEN McFEELY PRODUCED BY MARK JOHNSON PHILIP STEUER DIRECTED BY ANDREW ADAMSON Walt Disney Pictures

Narnia.com

0-00-722575-X

Printed and bound in Spain

THE CHRONICLES OF NARNIA

THE LION, THE WITCH AND THE WARDROBE

STORY AND ACTIVITY BOOK

HarperCollins *Children's Books*

CONTENTS

witch's castle

E T T I

n

a

R

Beaver's
dam

the Great River

allies'
enclave

rock
bridge

w

woods

frozen
lake

frozen
water

father
christmas

telmar river

shuddering
wood

che

·THE CHRONICLES OF·
NARNIA
THE LION, THE WITCH AND
THE WARDROBE

THE MOVIE STORY

Adapted by Kate Egan

Based on the screenplay
by Ann Peacock and Andrew Adamson
and Christopher Markus & Stephen McFeely

Based on the book by C. S. Lewis

Directed by Andrew Adamson

HarperCollins *Children's Books*

With air raids every night, wartime London was no place for children. So Mrs Pevensie decided her four children would wait out the war in the countryside. "It's just for a little while," she promised as they boarded a train.

Peter, the oldest, looked at his sisters and brother. "We've got to stick together now," he said. Susan, Edmund and Lucy stared back at him glumly. Nobody wanted to go where they were going – wherever it was.

A stern woman named Mrs Macready met them at the station. She worked for their host, Professor Kirke, and enforced all the rules at his huge, dark house. No shouting. No running. No sliding on the banisters. Life was quiet at the Professor's house. And deadly boring – especially on a rainy day.

Lucy suggested playing hide-and-seek. Peter had counted all the way up to ninety-six before she found a place to hide. In a rush, Lucy plunged into the magnificent wooden wardrobe that stood in a room of its own. She backed into it as far as she could go. Then suddenly she felt snow crunching beneath her feet!

Lucy was in the middle of a snow-covered forest! She made
her way through the icy trees, towards a faint light in the distance, and
found herself in a clearing beside a lamppost. Just when she was wondering
what to do next, she heard footsteps behind her. Lucy was being followed by
a creature who was half man, half goat. He was a Faun!

The Faun's name was Mr Tumnus. It turned out he was more afraid
of Lucy than Lucy was of him. And Lucy couldn't resist his invitation for tea
– she was dying to get out of the cold. On the way to his house, Lucy
discovered that she was in a land called Narnia, where it had been winter for
the last one hundred years.

"Winter's all right," Lucy said, trying to sound cheerful. "You can ice skate
and have snowball fights. And Christmas!"

Mr Tumnus shook his head. "Not here," he replied sadly. "We haven't had
Christmas for a hundred years."

Beside the Faun's blazing fire, Lucy ate all the tea cakes she could. But Mr Tumnus seemed scared when she decided to leave. "If I let you go, she'll turn me to stone," he whispered. "The White Witch! She's the one who makes it always winter. She gave orders . . . if we ever find a Human in the woods, we're supposed to turn it over to her."

Mr Tumnus broke the rules by helping her leave. Lucy just hoped he wouldn't get caught.

When she stepped back through the wardrobe, Lucy found that no time had passed at all. Nobody believed her story, either. That night, she crept down the hall with a candle and slipped back into Narnia. And this time Edmund followed her.

Edmund lost Lucy in the snow right away. But soon he met an elegant woman wrapped in fur, riding in a sleigh pulled by reindeer. She stopped when she saw him. "Pray, how did you come to enter my dominion?" she asked in an angry voice.

Nervously, Edmund stammered, "I-I-I'm not sure. . . . Lucy's the only one of us four who's been here before. . . . She said she met some Faun called T-T-Tumnus."

Suddenly the woman was friendlier. She conjured treats for Edmund – including his favourite, Turkish Delight! She told Edmund she was a Queen, and then she made him a tantalizing promise. One day, she might make him a Prince of Narnia – if only he would introduce her to his brother and sisters.

Edmund said good-bye to the nice Queen and watched her ride off in her sleigh. Moments later, he heard footsteps behind him. It was Lucy. "I told you Narnia was real!" she cried.

Lucy told him where she'd been. "I saw Mr Tumnus," she explained. "He's fine. The White Witch hasn't found out anything about him meeting me." Edmund froze. He looked down at the sleigh tracks in the snow. "Are you all right?" Lucy asked. "You look awful."

"What do you expect? I'm freezing. How do we get out of here?"

To Peter and Susan, Edmund pretended there was no such thing as Narnia. Even when Lucy had cried and begged her siblings to believe her, Edmund still denied it. But then one day he accidentally hit a cricket ball through a window at the Professor's house. Mrs Macready came running to check out the damage. The four kids were cornered – until they crammed into the wardrobe. When they wandered through the coats and felt the wet snow beneath their feet, everyone knew Lucy was telling the truth. "You little liar," Peter said to Edmund, threateningly.

The others hardly spoke to Edmund as they plodded through the snow to visit Mr Tumnus. But soon they had a bigger problem on their hands. The Faun's house was ruined – and Mr Tumnus was gone!

Lucy was sure it was her fault. What if Mr Tumnus had been turned to stone? She was determined to find him. Then two talking Beavers appeared to help!

"There is hope, dear," Mrs Beaver
assured her.

"There is more than hope," her husband
interrupted. "Aslan is on the move! He's the
King of the whole wood. He's the real King
of Narnia! And he's waiting for you at the
Stone Table!"

The Pevensies had no idea what he meant.

So the Beavers filled them in. Everything that was happening in Narnia – from Mr Tumnus's arrest to Aslan's return – was because of them. An ancient prophecy dictated that when two Sons of Adam and two Daughters of Eve – also known as Human children – arrived in Narnia, Aslan would come back!

With him, they would lead an army against the White Witch and restore peace to the land. Then they would ascend to four thrones in a palace called Cair Paravel!

None of it made any sense to Susan. There were no such things as Witches. She didn't care to be a Queen. She just wanted to go home.

It was much too late to leave, though. While the Beavers were talking to them, Edmund had run away to join the White Witch!

Peter, Susan and Lucy ran after him until the Beavers set them straight. If they followed their brother, they would walk straight into the hands of the Witch – who was waiting to pounce. They would have to go directly to Aslan. He was the only one who could help Edmund now.

Lucy hated to abandon her brother. And it was an awfully long way to the Stone Table, over a frozen river and through a dense forest. Even worse, the Witch's Wolves were on their trail!

Suddenly she heard them. Lucy flew into the woods, diving after Peter, Susan and the Beavers into a small cave. Soon she could hear sleigh bells right outside. It had to be the Witch herself!

Mr Beaver peeped out to get a look at her. But the Witch wasn't there. Instead it was Father Christmas, driving eight reindeer!

"I thought there was no Christmas in Narnia," said Susan suspiciously.

Father Christmas smiled. "Not for a long time," he said. "But the hope you have brought us, your Majesties, is finally weakening the Witch's magic. Still, you could probably do with these."

Father Christmas handed each of them
magnificent gifts.

Peter received a sword and a scabbard,
with a shield emblazoned with a lion.

Susan received a bow and a
quiver of arrows, plus an ivory horn.
Father Christmas promised that whenever she
blew it, help would come her way.

And Lucy received both a tiny dagger and a
jewelled vial containing the juice of the fireflower.
One drop of it would cure any injury.

Then Father Christmas flew
off across the snow, crying,
"Long live Aslan! And Merry
Christmas!" He was gone in
the blink of an eye.

Meanwhile, Edmund was in the Witch's clutches. There was no Turkish Delight for him at her castle. He wasn't about to become a Prince. Instead, the Witch was furious that Edmund had failed to deliver his brother and sisters. And she was angrier still when she found out they were looking for Aslan! If the children met up with the King, her reign would be in jeopardy. She would simply have to stop them!

The Witch strapped Edmund into her sleigh and went off in search of
Peter, Susan and Lucy. She found the Fox who'd promised to guide them to
the Stone Table – and she turned him into stone. Then the Witch ordered
her Wolves to head off the children at the river.

Peter, Susan and Lucy had to get across the frozen river without the help of the Fox. It was hard to believe, but it seemed as if the river was beginning to melt.

Great cracks opened up in the ice as they
rushed across. And then they were ambushed by
the Witch's Wolves! The chief Wolf, Maugrim,
promised that Peter's family would be safe if only
they left Narnia at once. Peter wanted to believe him.
At the same time, though, other Wolves were growling
at the Beavers.

Peter didn't know what to do. He didn't like to fight.
He just wanted to have some peace.

Maugrim howled and prepared to tear him to pieces.

Just then, though, a waterfall above them gave way. Chunks of ice pounded the Wolves, and a torrent of water washed the children away!

When they landed on the shore of the river, shivering and wet, they all noticed a change in the air. They could actually feel the warm sun on their skin. Lucy pointed at the flowers popping out of the earth. Even Susan had to admit something miraculous was happening. Spring was coming to Narnia!

The White Witch had to admit it, too. Her sleigh was stuck in the mud! If she was ever going to keep the Pevensies from reaching Aslan, she would have to go on foot. Wearily, Edmund trudged behind her.

The Beavers and the Pevensies made their way through the forest and came into a large clearing. There, a Centaur standing guard saw them and sounded a horn. A cluster of leaves swirled into the air, taking the form of a pair of Dryads who bowed to the children. As the party stepped forward, a magnificent sight sprawled before them – it was Aslan's camp.

The bustling creatures of the camp grew silent as the children and the
Beavers moved through the crowd. There in the centre of the camp was a
huge tent. As they argued over who would go in first, the tent flap opened
and the children fell silent, too. Before them stood a fearsome and beautiful
golden Lion, his mane shimmering in the sun. It was Aslan.

Aslan welcomed the three children warmly. But then he asked, "Where is the fourth?"

The Pevensies explained how Edmund had betrayed them to the Witch, how they loved him anyway because he was their brother and how they needed Aslan's help if they were ever to find him.

Aslan listened carefully and said, "All shall be done for Edmund."

Later, Peter took a walk alone with Aslan. The Lion showed him Cair Paravel, glittering in the distance, where someday he was to sit as the High King.

Peter wasn't sure he could do it. He wasn't even sure he wanted to. He'd had a hard enough time keeping his family safe. How could he ever be a King?

Aslan said, "Peter, I will do all I can to help your family. But I need you to consider what I ask of you." He pointed at his bustling camp and added, "I, too, want my family safe."

If he was ever to deliver Edmund from the Witch's grasp, Peter would have to deliver Narnia from her grasp, too. He would have to help fight her forces. He would have to fulfill the prophecy.

Suddenly Wolves sneaked up on Susan and Lucy, who were bathing in a river. A Centaur, Oreius, rushed to help the girls – until Aslan stopped him. "No, Oreius, let the young Prince fight this battle," he said.

This time Peter drew his sword without hesitating. This time he fought – both for Narnia and for Edmund. And this time Maugrim was killed.

That night Centaurs slipped into the Witch's camp and rescued Edmund. Aslan brought him to the other children at dawn, instructing, "There is no need to speak to Edmund about what is past." They weren't quite ready to forgive their brother, but nobody dared to defy Aslan.

Now that they were all together, Susan
wanted to go home. After all, she pointed out,
this was a war just like the one their mother
wanted to protect them from. But Peter knew
what he had to do now. And Edmund under-
stood the Witch's strength. The four of them
would have to fight her forces. They
would have to get ready for battle.

Then they learned that Aslan had agreed to meet with the Witch. She arrived in a procession of monsters and snarled, "You have a traitor amongst you, Aslan. And every traitor belongs to me."

Aslan and the Witch spoke alone. When they were through, Aslan announced to the crowd, "She has renounced her claim on Edmund's blood." He sealed the deal with a mighty roar, and the Witch marched away.

War still loomed, but Edmund was safe.

That night, Lucy was lying awake when she saw Aslan's shadow move past her tent. She and Susan followed him to the Stone Table, which was lit by torches and surrounded by the Witch and her monsters. They taunted and tormented the Lion. They teased and poked him. And then they killed him! Susan and Lucy could hardly believe their eyes.

Back in the camp, Peter heard the terrible news. Now it seemed impossible for him to do what Aslan had asked.

But Edmund encouraged him. "Aslan chose you to lead his army," he reminded his brother. "That army is ready to follow you. And so am I!"

Suddenly Peter felt a little braver. "Tell the troops that we will meet the Witch in battle without Aslan," he commanded Oreius.

On a white Unicorn, Peter headed for the battlefield.

At the sound of a trumpet, the Witch's army stormed onto the field. It was a teeming mass of all the evil creatures known to Narnia. Peter's army was completely outnumbered.

Peter rode to the front of his troops and took a deep breath. The army was attentive – but silent. "For Narnia! For Aslan!" he cried. The troops exploded into applause, clanging their swords against their shields.

And Peter led the charge towards the Witch's army!

Susan and Lucy were grief stricken. They couldn't bear to leave Aslan's body even if the battle was beginning. But suddenly they heard a strange rumbling, and then a sound like thunder and an earthquake all at once. When the shaking subsided, they found that the Stone Table had been split in two . . . and Aslan himself stood before them!

The Witch's magic was powerful, he explained. But there was something more powerful than even she knew: the difference between right and wrong. When a Narnian created as much wrong as the Witch did, even death could be overturned!

The girls climbed on Aslan's back and galloped across the countryside to the melting ruins of the Witch's ice castle. In the courtyard they found the stone statues the Witch had created with her dark magic – and one of them was Mr Tumnus! Aslan breathed on the Faun until he came back to life. The Lion did the same for the thousands of other statues. Then he led them back to the battlefield – and not a moment too soon.

Peter's army was on the verge of collapse. The Witch had turned many of his soldiers to stone. She was now closing in on Peter, her wand raised. Seeing this, Edmund brought down his sword and smashed the wand in two. Furious, the White Witch let out a horrible scream. She wounded Edmund with what was left of her wand and he fell to the ground.

Aslan bounded down a cliff directly towards her. He pounced and roared –
and then the Witch was gone, with one flash of his mighty teeth!

A Dwarf stood poised over Edmund, ready to finish him off . . . but Susan
felled him with one of her arrows. Then Lucy took out her jewelled vial. She
healed Edmund first, then the other soldiers, one by one.

Their work on the battlefield was done. Now it was time for the Pevensies to be crowned at Cair Paravel!

Peter, Susan, Edmund and Lucy sat upon their new thrones and beamed as Aslan pronounced them the new Kings and Queens of Narnia. A great celebration began in the ancient castle . . . and only Lucy noticed the Lion slipping away.

Fifteen years later, the Kings and Queens set off in search of the famous White Stag. They tore off after it into the woods until the branches gave way and they found themselves . . . in a wardrobe.

They realised no time at all had passed since they entered the wardrobe. The Kings and Queens were children again, back inside the Professor's house.

That night Lucy crept back to the room with the wardrobe.

Suddenly she heard a sound. She wheeled around and found the Professor there, shaking his head. "I'm afraid you won't get back in that way. I already tried."

"Will we ever go back?" Lucy asked sadly.

And the Professor answered, "I should think so. But it'll likely happen when you're not looking for it. All the same . . . best to keep your eyes open."

Scrambled Journal

Susan is writing in her diary about the creatures of Narnia, but she's scrambling their names in case the White Witch finds it. Unscramble the words below to discover their names.

ASLAN

1) LNASA
2) VEREAB
3) NUFA
4) TRECAUN
5) ROCNINU
6) FDWAR
7) ERGO
8) TINGA

TEA WITH MR TUMNUS

Lucy joins her new friend, Mr Tumnus, for tea and sardines.

THE ESCAPE

The Pevensie children are leaving London for the Professor's house,
but Edmund and Peter have fallen behind. Help them find their way through
the house to the carriage where Susan and Lucy are waiting for them.

FINISH

A WARDROBE WITH A VIEW

While trying to hide from Mrs Macready, all four Pevensie children end up in Narnia. Using the picture below as a guide, draw your own picture of Narnia.

MAKING SQUARES

You'll need a friend to play this game. Each player takes turns connecting
the images of Mr Tumnus, one line at a time, to make a square.
When you complete a square, put your initial in it. You can use your
opponent's lines to make a square. The player with the most squares wins!

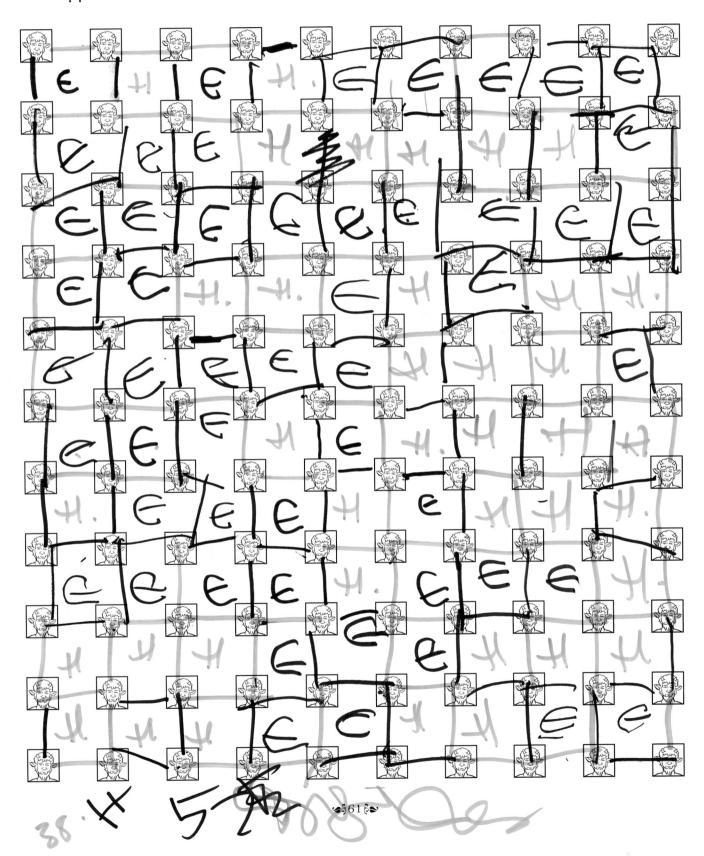

THE WORLD BEYOND THE WARDROBE

"I'm sure it's just your imagination."

Fun in the Snow!

There's always time for a snowball fight – if you've just stumbled upon a magical world, that is! Count each Pevensie's pile of snowballs to find out who will win.

SKETCH PAD

On Lucy's first trip to Narnia, she met
Mr Tumnus, the Faun. Lucy thought Fauns were
only in books. Draw a creature that you've read
about in a book but never seen.

A Strange Encounter
with the White Witch

The White Witch impresses Edmund with her magical powers.
But something isn't quite right. Find at least twelve mistakes in the scene.

A MAGICAL VISIT

Lucy warms up in Mr Tumnus's cottage. While the Faun is fetching more firewood, Lucy takes a look around. Some of what she sees is hidden in the puzzle below. The words will appear forwards, backwards, up, down and diagonally.

FIND:

BOOKS

FIREPLACE

FIREWOOD

HANDKERCHIEF

KNICKKNACKS

PAINTINGS

POTS

SARDINES

SAUCER

TEA

TEACUP

TOAST

TRUNK

```
P  E  S  A  R  D  I  N  E  S  B  X
F  I  R  E  P  L  A  C  E  A  O  E
X  R  E  C  U  A  S  D  P  L  O  I
S  K  C  A  N  K  K  C  I  N  K  C
F  I  R  E  W  O  O  D  E  O  S  D
E  I  O  T  G  C  Q  A  P  P  G  R
X  P  P  E  S  Y  T  P  U  J  O  Q
K  A  O  P  M  O  E  C  X  T  K  K
N  E  U  T  A  Q  A  F  G  P  O  N
U  I  R  S  S  E  Z  O  O  K  E  A
R  H  T  A  T  P  G  A  L  Q  R  P
T  P  S  G  N  I  T  N  I  A  P  E
F  E  I  H  C  R  E  K  D  N  A  H
```

SOMETHING IN THE DISTANCE

Edmund stumbles through the wardrobe and finds himself all alone in Narnia.
But he soon sees someone approaching. Could it be Lucy?
Connect the dots and find out!

THE OFFICIAL NOTICE

When Peter, Susan, Edmund and Lucy arrive at Mr Tumnus's house, they're surprised to find a message tacked to the door. What has happened to Mr Tumnus? Solve the maths problems below to find out. When you're finished, fit the letters into the numbered spaces and read the scroll.

_h_ F_u_ _u__us is h___by
5 20   21 19   5 24 19   20 3 20

ch__ged wi_h High ____s__
21 3   5   5 3 20 21 8 19

_g_i_s_ h__ I_p__i_l
21 21 19 5 20 3 24 20 3 21

____s_y __dis, Qu___ _f
24 21 23 20 5 23 21   20 20 19 8

____i_, f__ c__f___i_g
19 21 3 19 21 8 3 8 24 8 3 5 19

h__ ____ies __d
20 3 20 19 20 24 21 19

f_____izi_g wi_h hu___s.
3 21 5 20 3 19 19   5   24 21 19

J = 4+19   O = 12-4   T = 15÷3   E = 2x10

N = 15+4   A = 30-9   R = 18÷6   M = 6x4

WATER FIGHT!

Susan and Lucy are having a water fight in the river. But something is not right.
Fill in the vowels A, E, I, O or U in the spaces below to find out what's wrong.

M_ _GR_M _S H_D_NG

B_H_ND TH_ TR_ _!

CROSSWORD

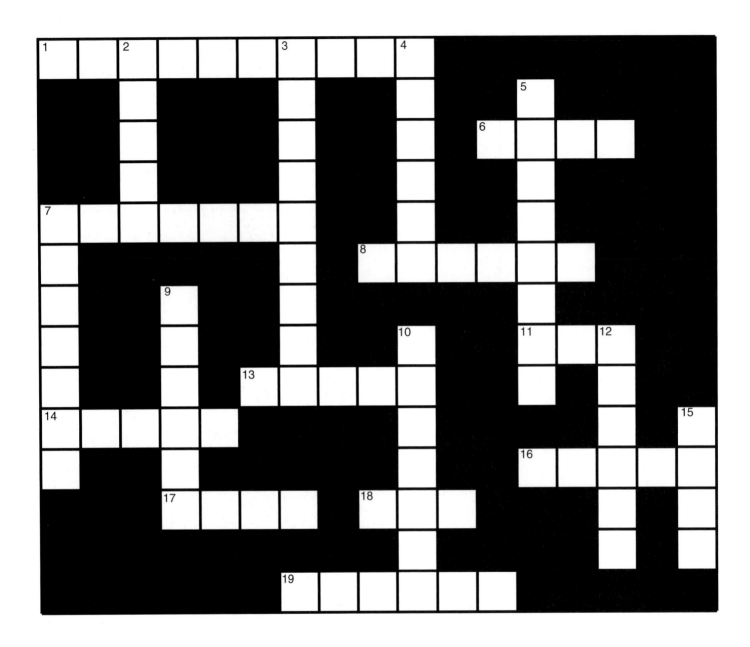

Across

1. The _____ of Narnia.

6. The Pevensies play in the snow by the _____post.

7. As Narnian royalty, the Pevensies get to sit on these.

8. This tree bears fruit and is the first to blossom again in Narnia.

11. Susan practises with her _____ and arrow.

13. The children must journey to find _____ and his army.

14. Aslan's camp is near the _____ Table.

16. The oldest Pevensie.

17. The youngest Pevensie.

18. A clever friend of the Pevensies.

19. Lucy's first friend in Narnia.

Down

2. The ice starts to break up while the children are crossing the _____.

3. Father _____ hasn't been seen in Narnia for a long time.

4. The Witch rides in one of these.

5. To get to Narnia, the Pevensies go through one of these.

7. Edmund's favourite sweet is _____ Delight.

9. The Beavers help Peter, Susan and Lucy escape through one of these.

10. A one-horned creature of Narnia.

12. For the past hundred years, it's been this season in Narnia.

15. Peter leads the Narnian _____ into battle.

START
1

FINISH

974

STARRY SKIES

Edmund is busy looking at the stars while his siblings are inside the Beavers' lodge.
Can you connect the dots and figure out what he sees?

THE STONE GARDEN

When Edmund finally reaches the White Witch's castle, he sees a shocking sight.
Hundreds of creatures have been frozen in stone. Find and circle the eleven
differences between these two pictures.

HELP FROM A FRIEND

After the Pevensies and the Beavers make their way through the winding tunnel, they find themselves in need of some help. Luckily for them, a friend is ready to distract Maugrim. Connect the dots and reveal their secret ally.

THE FIRST SIGNS OF SPRING

Peter, Susan and Lucy can't believe their eyes when they find a cherry tree blossoming in the middle of the frozen forest.

THE GIFTS

Father Christmas has something special for Peter, Susan and Lucy.
Unscramble the words below to find out what he brings for them.

1. _sword_
   WDORS

2. _____
   VREIQU FO OWRSAR

3. _bow_
   OWB

4. _____
   NIYT ERGGAD

5. _____
   LWEELEJD IAVL

THE WOLVES ARE COMING

Once Edmund tells their secret to the White Witch, his siblings are in grave danger.
Help Peter, Susan, Lucy and the Beavers escape from the White Witch's Wolves!

START

FINISH

SLY FOX

Mr Fox outsmarted the Wolves and saved Peter, Susan and Lucy. But can he outsmart you? Look closely at the six pictures below. Which picture is different?

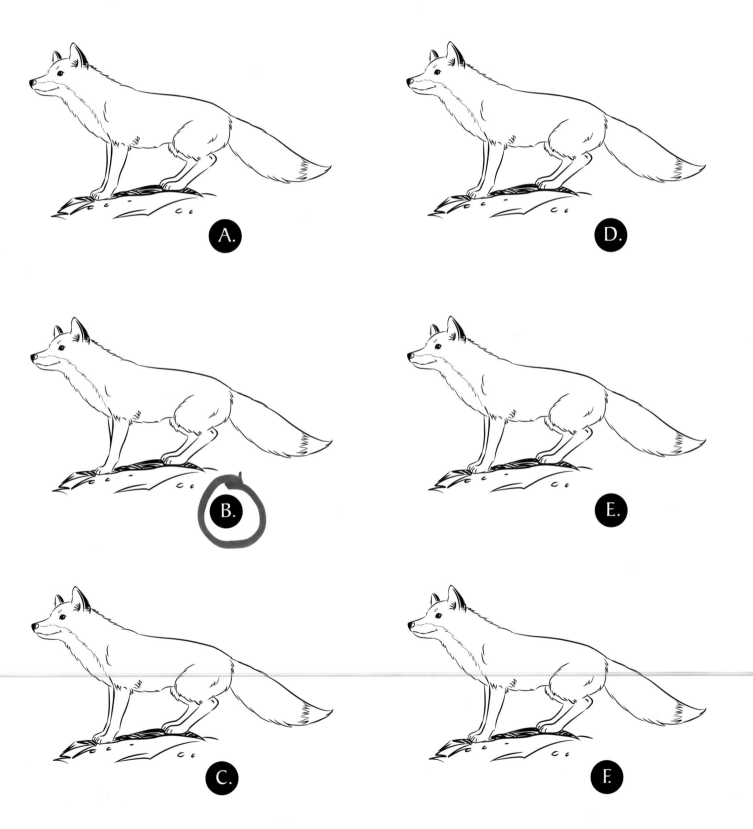

A.

D.

B.

E.

C.

F.

BATTLE ON ICE

Nature takes over when Maugrim and the other wolves
catch up to the Pevensies in the middle of a frozen river.

THE REUNION

Aslan is leading Edmund back to the camp. Follow the odd numbers in the puzzle up, down, left and right to help Edmund begin his journey back to his siblings. Then follow the even numbers to help all four Pevensies make their way to the field, where they need to prepare for tomorrow's battle.

START	3	24	44	96	2	91	125	27	101	72
	19	18	88	42	14	47	76	62	95	90
	23	36	34	18	133	95	32	49	17	50
	65	49	62	22	17	36	10	77	32	78
	38	31	94	35	69	104	90	55	46	118
	7	97	56	107	30	52	34	27	83	9
	71	34	80	5	104	134	8	70	38	111
	63	97	22	37	12	92	10	74	84	95
	24	45	63	29	126	148	84	40	6	43
	82	106	96	54	62	122	100	112	144	67 FINISH

START	48	45	56	30	12	17	35	105	43	9
	62	53	102	63	18	51	60	42	38	25
	4	36	98	3	144	93	52	71	62	64
	39	99	85	91	112	5	48	7	53	38
	113	48	8	136	120	81	136	117	92	56
	29	50	73	15	107	69	94	77	30	79
	123	88	27	110	138	144	6	23	16	11
	61	36	121	42	59	133	33	103	42	115
	75	22	90	38	125	49	131	55	90	104
	13	87	111	95	31	101	21	127	41	122 FINISH

A SHADOW IN THE NIGHT

Susan and Lucy awake to see a shadow of a figure walking past their tent. But who would be leaving the camp at this hour? Connect the dots to find out.

THE FINAL BATTLE

Look carefully at these two battle scenes. They may look the same at first glance, but there are fourteen differences between the two. Circle the differences.

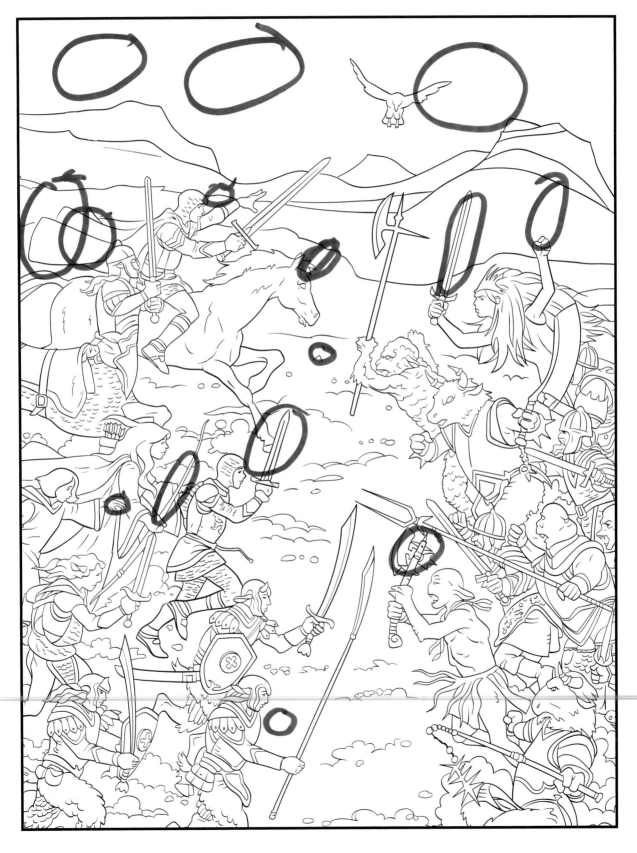

THE GREAT RETURN

Aslan has sacrificed himself for Edmund and has miraculously come back to life. Help Aslan, Susan and Lucy free the imprisoned creatures from the Witch's stone garden and then join the army to help Peter and Edmund before it's too late.

START

FINISH

A Sad Farewell

Before Aslan leaves Narnia, he bestows titles on the Pevensie children, making them the new Kings and Queens of Narnia. Unscramble the words below to find out each child's new title.

king Peter the magnificant

GNKI REETP HET NFAMIECGITN

UENEQ ASNUS TEH LTEGNE

king Edm

GKIN MDNUED EHT SUJT

EENUQ CYLU HET LAIVNAT

GOOD-BYE ASLAN

It is time for the Great Lion to leave Narnia once again.
Using this picture as a guide, draw your own picture of Aslan opposite.

ANSWERS

Page 55: SCRAMBLED JOURNAL

1) ASLAN
2) BEAVER
3) FAUN
4) CENTAUR
5) UNICORN
6) DWARF
7) OGRE
8) GIANT

Pages 58-59: THE ESCAPE

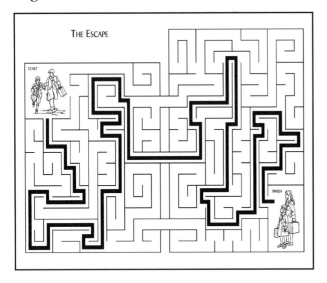

Page 64: FUN IN THE SNOW!

LUCY WINS! SHE HAS 22 SNOWBALLS;
PETER HAS 16; EDMUND HAS 14 AND
SUSAN HAS 21.

Pages 66-67: A STRANGE ENCOUNTER WITH THE WHITE WITCH

Page 68: A MAGICAL VISIT

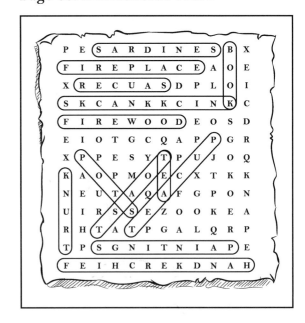

Page 70: THE OFFICIAL NOTICE

THE FAUN TUMNUS IS HEREBY
CHARGED WITH HIGH TREASON
AGAINST HER IMPERIAL
MAJESTY JADIS, QUEEN OF
NARNIA, FOR COMFORTING
HER ENEMIES AND
FRATERNIZING WITH HUMANS.

Pages 72-73: CROSSWORD

ANSWERS

Page 76: STONE GARDEN

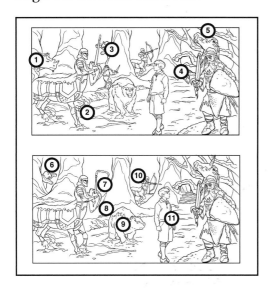

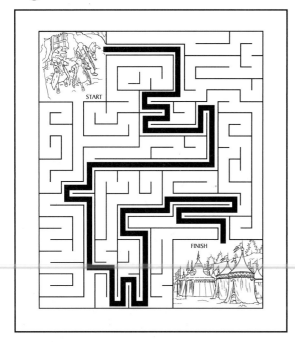

Page 79: THE GIFTS

1. SWORD
2. QUIVER OF ARROWS
3. BOW
4. TINY DAGGER
5. JEWELLED VIAL

Page 80: THE WOLVES ARE COMING

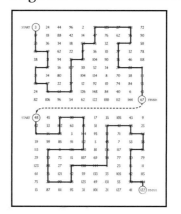

Page 81: SLY FOX

THE ANSWER IS B

Page 84: THE REUNION

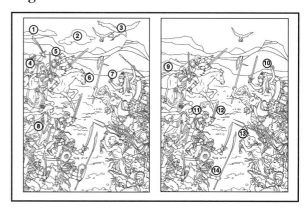

Pages 86-87: THE FINAL BATTLE

Page 88: THE GREAT RETURN

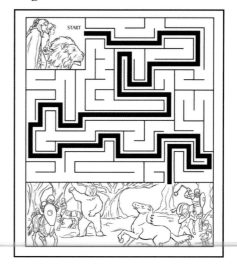

Page 89: A SAD FAREWELL

KING PETER THE MAGNIFICENT
KING EDMUND THE JUST
QUEEN SUSAN THE GENTLE
QUEEN LUCY THE VALIANT

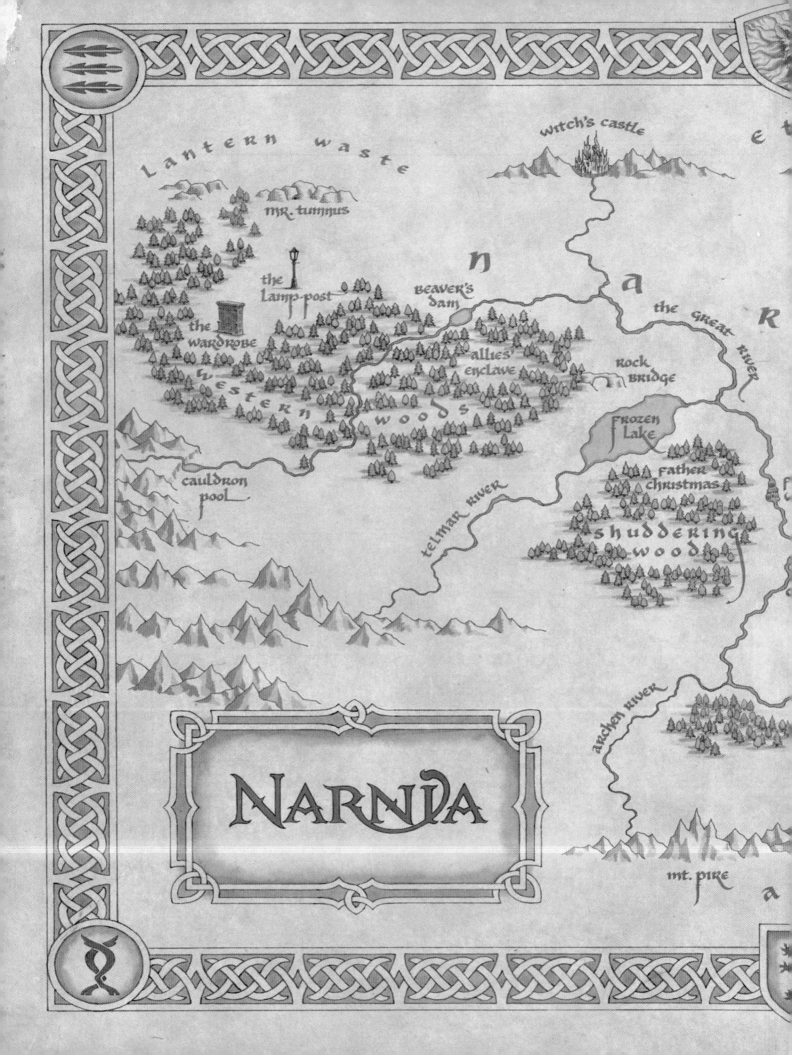